The One-Winged Body

Published by Marrowstone Press © 2025, *All rights reserved*

ISBN: 979-8-218-85259-7

The One-Winged Body

Photographs
Galen Garwood

Poems
Peter Weltner

Second Edition

MARROWSTONE

CONTENTS

After Pan

Ronnie discovered it, half-hidden by brambles, brush,
and weeds in a hill on the edge of old Ed Snyder's
corn field, a slit of a mouth in the earth, the cave,
dug or eroded from red clay long before the plague.
We were just wandering, two boys free, as we did
every summer day, not looking for a place to hide
from afternoon thunderstorms, inside stripping
bare naked, the glistening walls so hot they sweat.
Today, I received a photograph, shot in a Cretan
cave, of a young man with mane-like wavy black
hair, his thinly carved body boasting an erection
so fine it could have been aroused only by
a god's invocation: lightning, storms, fallen city
walls, men in ecstasy calling, crying for more love.

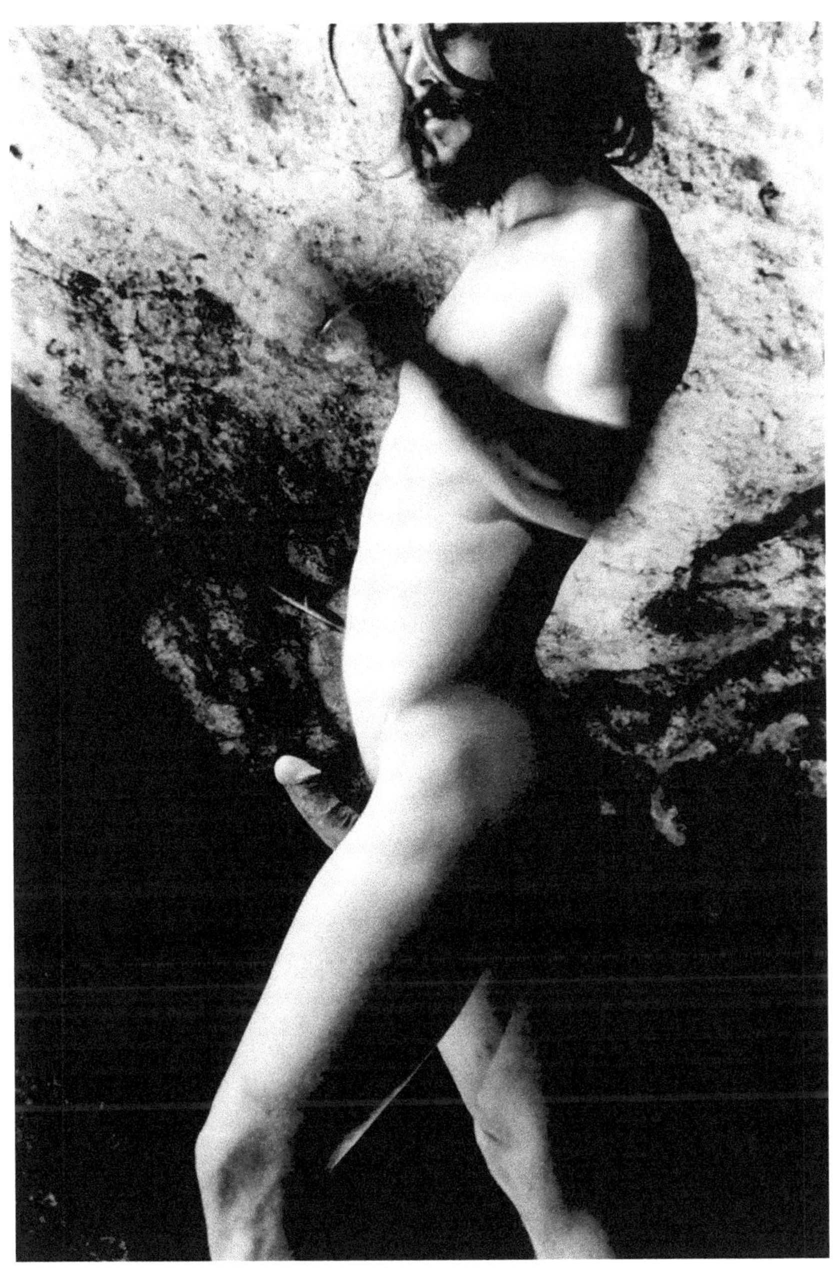

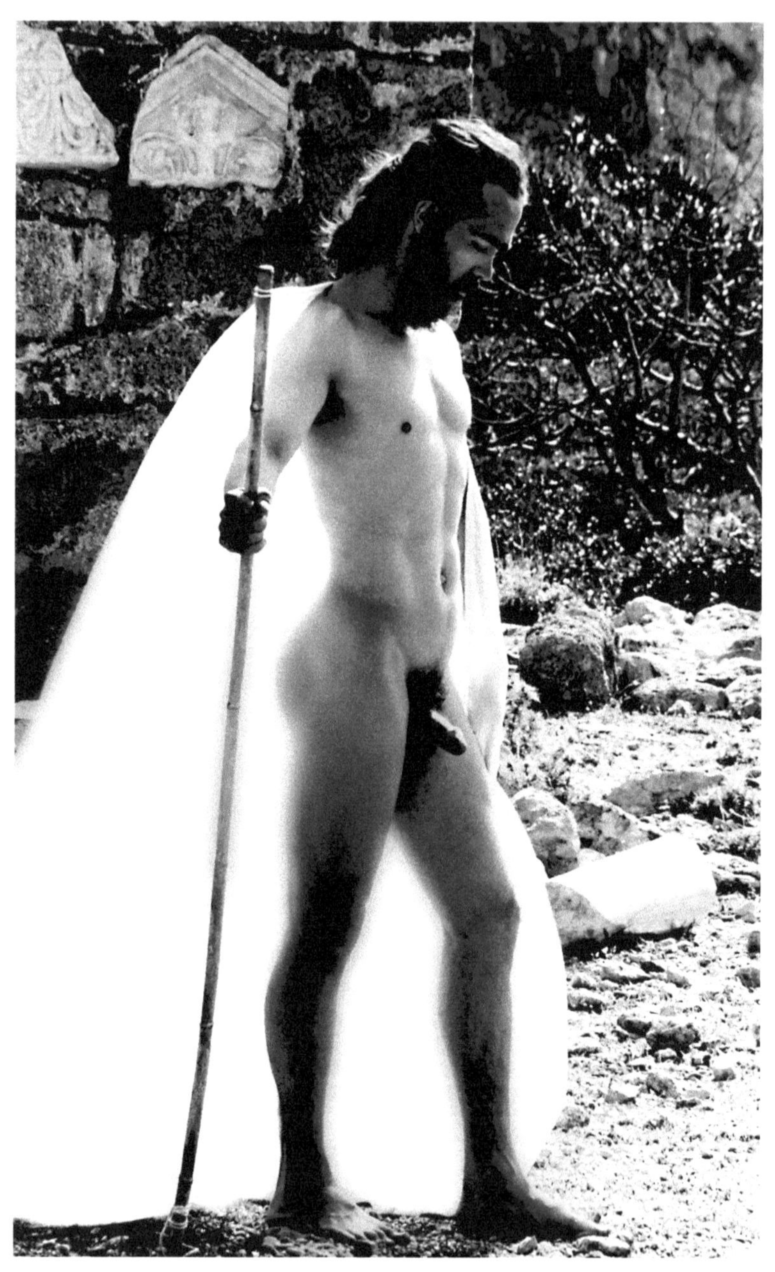

In Lissos

In Botticelli, wind-blown, Aphrodite steps ashore
out of Ouranos' shell. She cups her right hand
modestly over her right breast. Her left hand,
a swath of unshorn golden hair conceal her vulva.
Dressed in a gown dotted with cornflowers, a nymph
holds a daisy sown mantle to robe her nakedness.
But this is Lissos, 'Ninety-Six. The cloak
Galen's Christopher wears is a radiant cloud
dissolving into mist, a white light from which
he is being born, an archaic wild beauty,
a naked bearded kouros stepping onto rock,
ancient marble strewn ground. At night, he sleeps
under a sky said to have revealed to Plato: Men
die when time cannot love them as it loves itself.

Pan: Hania

Sixteen, I jackknifed off a board, hit my skull
on a rock in mud. The last thing I saw was the sun,
the lake I'm drowning in translucent as air.
Water man shadow dream. Wiping a mirror clean
of steam after a shower, dripping, erect, Bob
drops his towel. A full moon rains onto our bed.
In Crete, in an underwater room, a young
man plays his flute while just over his head
crests break, the surface rippling in lunar
light. The music he makes pleases his cock.
Fire, water. His desire's a torch that blazes
whitest when submerged, however dark the sea.
Dive to him. Water is freedom. Water is peace.
In the deep, gold gleams. Best of all things is water.

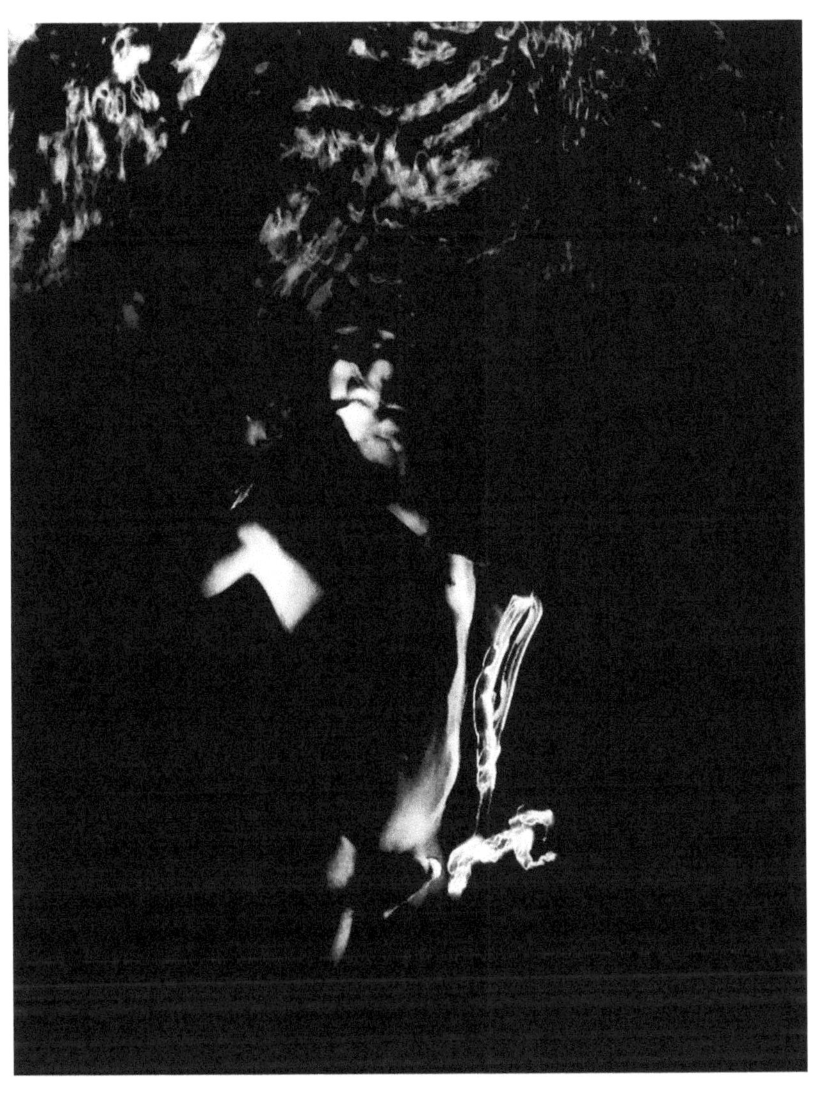

Rockface and Stream

He's retreated to wilderness, jagged rock face,
sparse trees, twig tangled dark pointillist leaves,
a stream, a sunlit cliff on the other side—an obscure
cool spot where a prophet might rest from heat.
He wears his clothes like a holy man's, waist
cinched, shoulder draped, lifts an arm to grieve.
Thirteen, I found hidden deep in a forest,
in a rhododendron thicket on a honeysuckle
sweetened slope below Hanging Rock, a cascade
and a naked man bathing in its pounding waters.
He's turned his face away. There's only his black
hair to see, his back, the curve of butt and thigh.
Flesh of his flesh, no words, no book to follow.
What will become of me when he turns round to look?

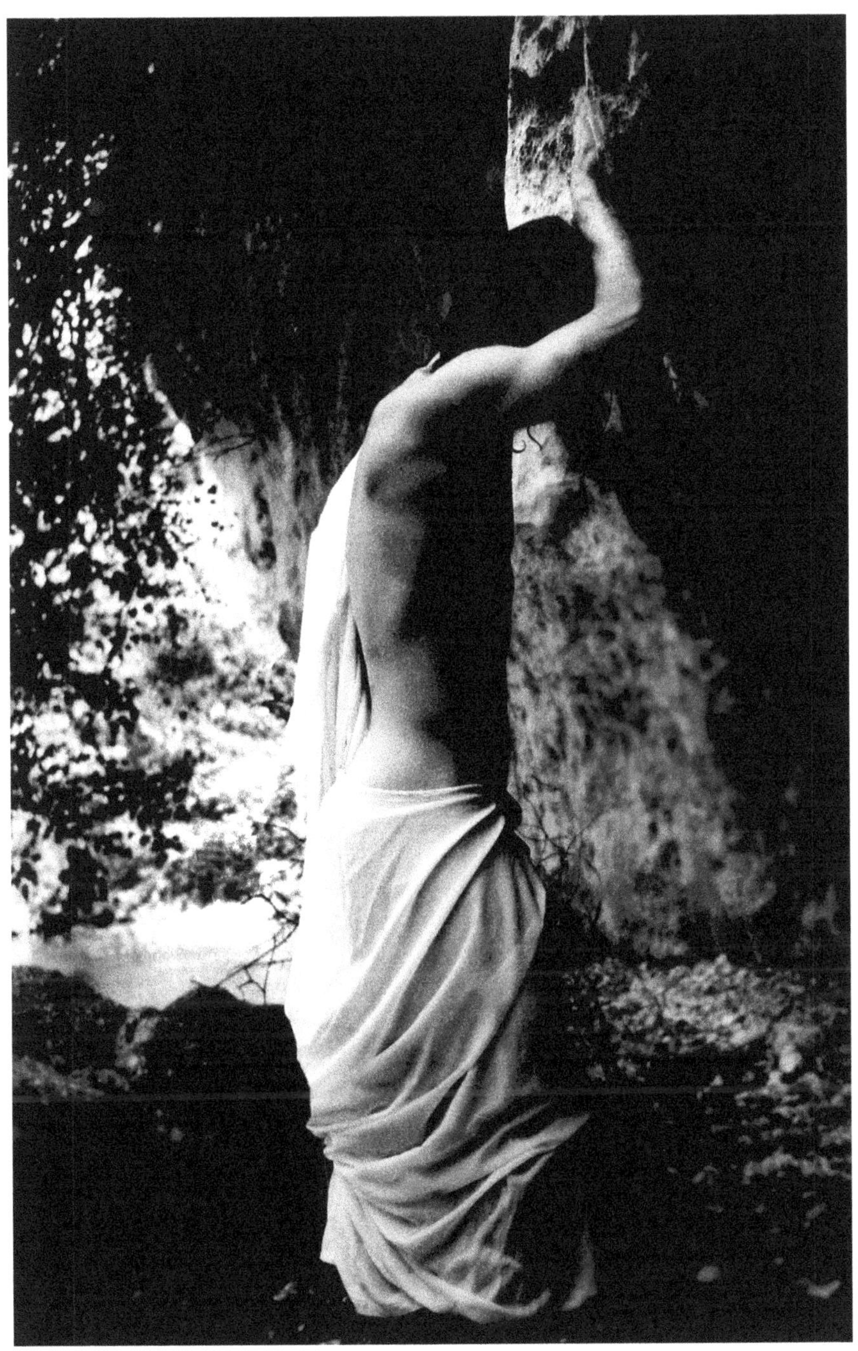

Temple Music

Not wisdom through suffering, but awe: men
felled at the whim of gods they're better than.
Bad weather. Sicily's more dark than light—
unsettled ashen skies over the coast.
Hera's temple's black ruins on a field
of sooty grass, weed scorched like charcoal.
The scene's grainy like a still from a surreal
silent film or a daguerrotype. A storm's coming.
A boy stands torso bared, his sheet-like skirt
billowing. The mask he wears shines faceless
as a crescent moon, hides what his chest boldly
exposes: a beauty to envy, disguised as a pose,
defiant, daring tragedy to live again, rise,
its wave-maddened horses, lascivious winds.

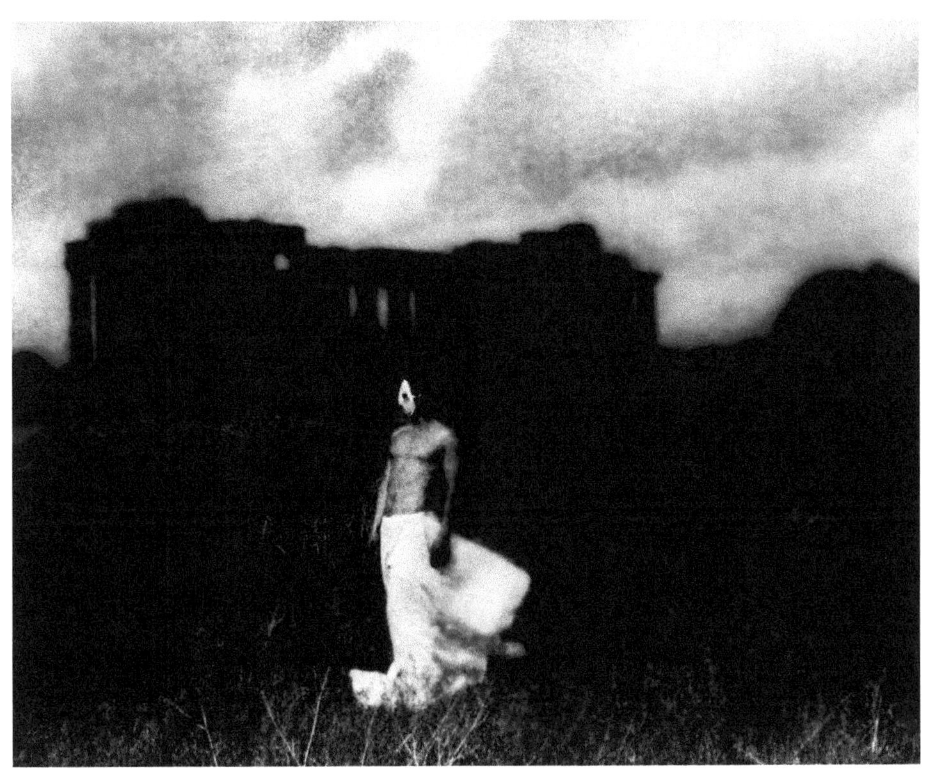

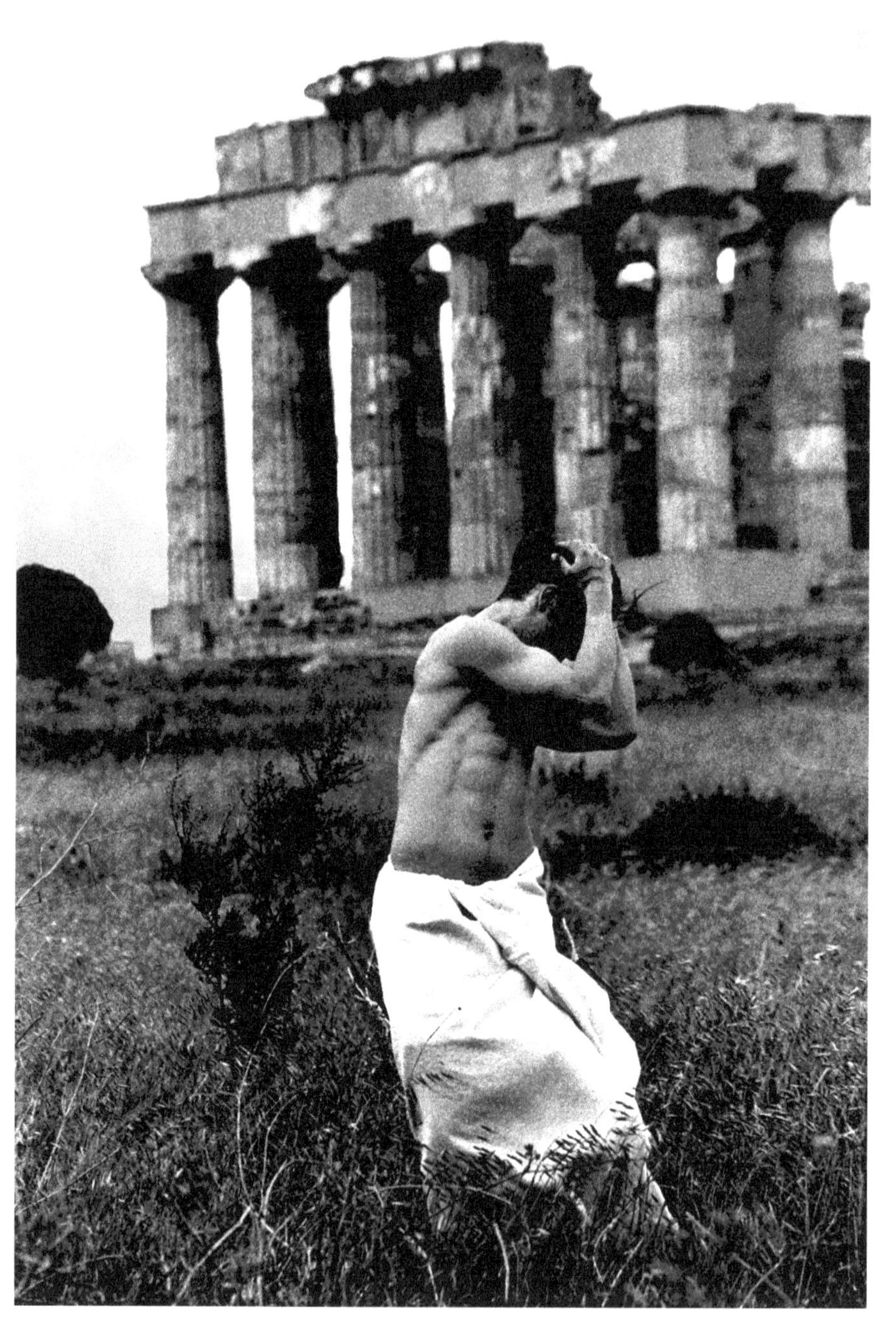

King Selinus

If we should peer beyond what is ours to see,
utter blasphemies by words and deeds,
never fear the gods, trespass sacred places,
profane the sea, sky, olive groves, grape vines,
pine, spirits of fruits of ivy, wild selino,
if we defy justice, stain the good with folly,
fail the feast days, lay hands on tainted
things, how might we dance or holily grieve?
The gods are long gone, their temples rubble
for millennia. Yet look how he turns his torso,
its tragic, classic form, how—no odes to sing—
he alone is left of the chorus, how his hands
grip his head and hair, how his muscles are taut with
sensual despair, no flute to follow, reverent of the rites.

Torso: Dionysos

This day, you need neither ivy, wine, panther,
pard, frenzied women nor earthquake to be
free, just primitive tricks of the prick. Quick
as that beloved becomes lover, your godhead
revealed. Close by is an olive grove, weathered
rock old as the island. The sun's high, delights
in your body, But your face is hidden, my lord,
though you've stripped off your royal loincloth
draped round your waist to show the black locks
below, your blood taut cock ecstasy's promise.
For the seed you'll spill into his sweating flesh
is sharp as snake's teeth, hot as a lion's breath,
white as goat's milk fresh from the teat, pungent
with earth—pine, stone, lichens, moss, fleshy loam.

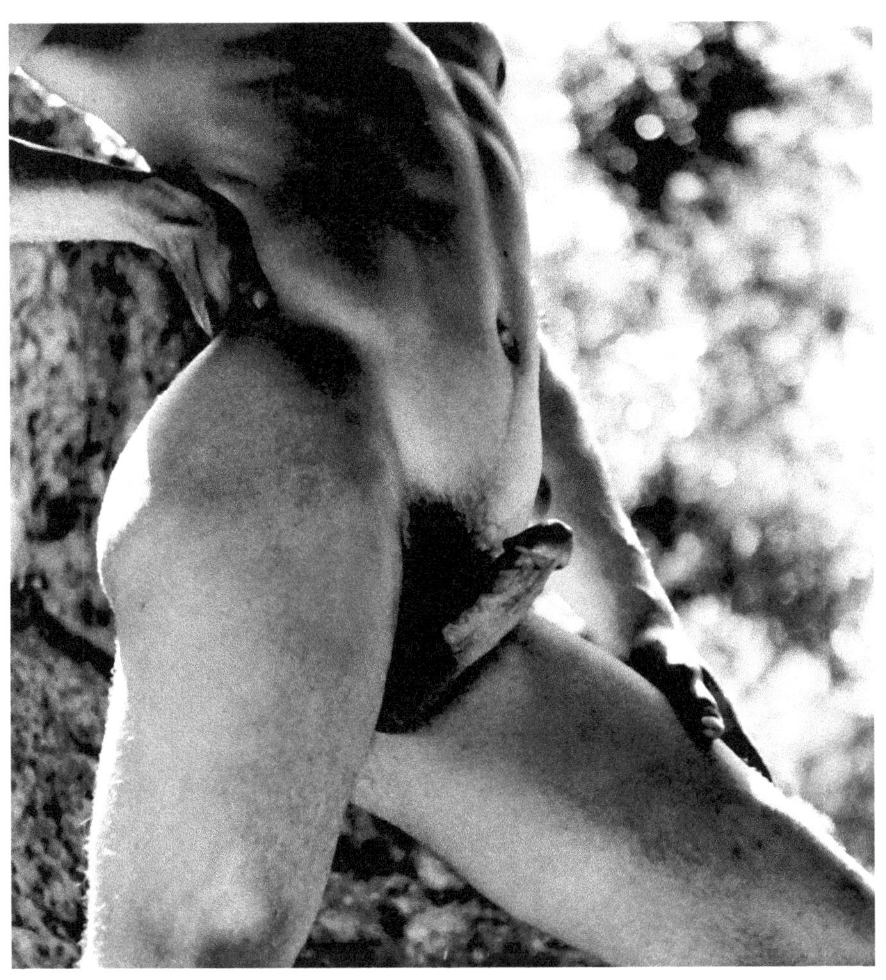

On Crete, in Athens

Why wear your spectral, gauzy cloth when you
can strip it off? On Crete, you're a Cretan boy
reborn, ready for bull leaping, a Minoan stone
figurine or vase found whole, not a shard. Sacred,
these groves, mountains, rocks, laurel, streams
where you walk. Dawn's burning through olive,
pine, rain's battering a boat, a hut, a temple's
fluted marble, winds, white water far out to sea,
divine footprints mysteriously imprinted on
the shore left to explore like driftwood or debris,
the sun's adoring naked skin proof enough then
the gods were real as you. Myth is free, history
ghost pale. Do you remember wrestling that last day
in the gymnasium, Kritias, Phaedus fighting over you?

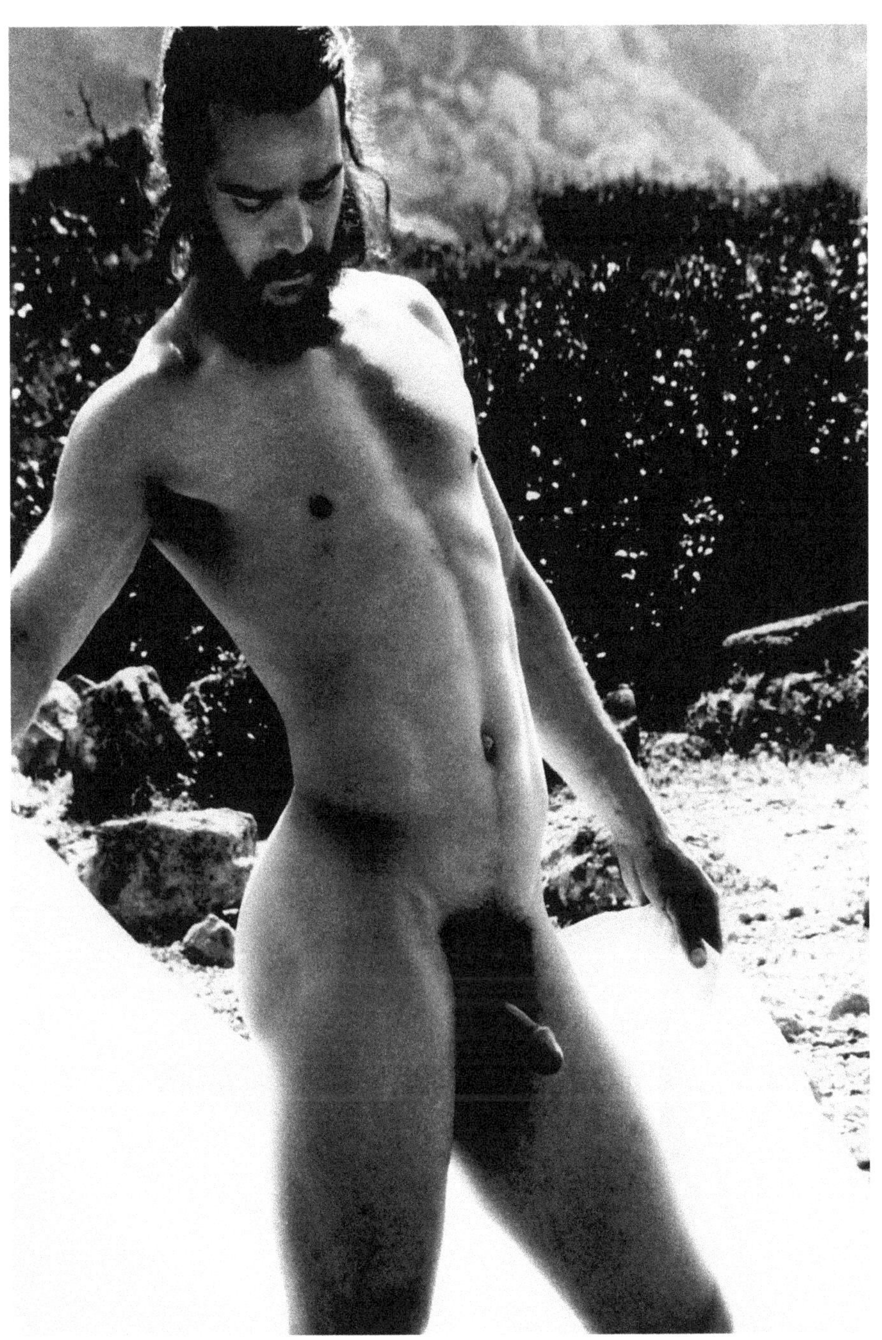

A Pool, a Lake

Though he's better looking, Robert and I, when
lovers, were often mistaken for brothers,
an illusion, a trick of the light, blurry vision.
He's taller, his hair's far fairer than mine,
his eyes blue, mine pale green. Not doubles
at all. Yet we could see what others saw,
as if each was a mirror of the other we dived
into like a glassy pool deep in obscure woods.
Water or light. You choose, Christopher. Pond,
lake where your body is reflected. Suppose
Narcissus saw in that shimmering mirror not
himself but his lover who rose out of water
like Venus after her father has spilled his seed
in the sea. His passion is what shines back as yours.

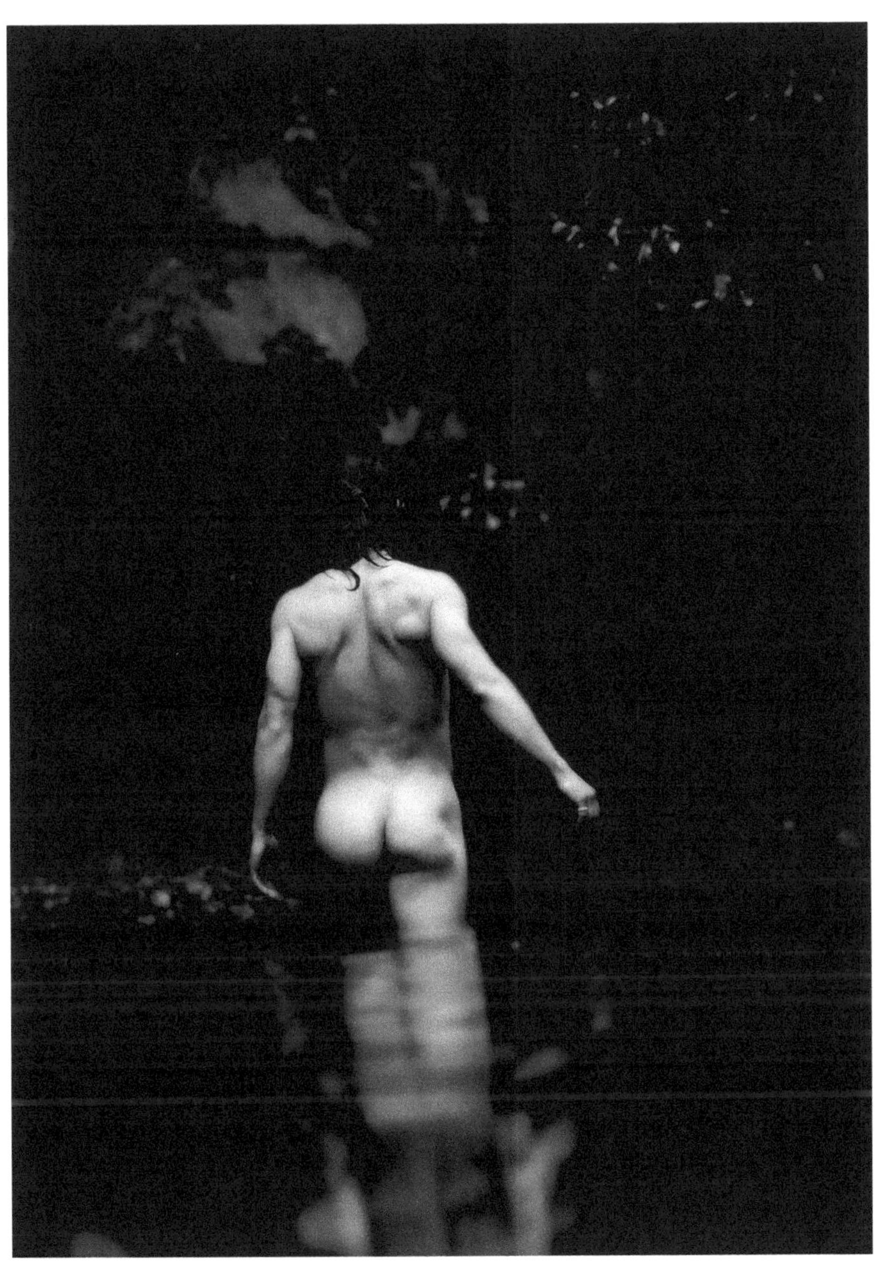

A Cemetery in Savannah

Traveler, you who pass by and wonder why,
know I lie where all my life I dread to be.
Fast as I fled from death, he chose to run
toward me. Let a boy's supple muscles, back,
shoulders, arms rhyme with my tomb cover's
curve. Beauty is never enough to save us,
never suffices to see us through. Even if he
seems a god's equal, time's arc is always the same.
The dead can't love nor can oblivion feel.
Fear of the end made Frankenstein try to
resurrect a corpse like mine. I'd be his monster
if I could. I'm anonymous, no lasting fame
despite my name. Read it stranger, and smile
even as your eyes dwell on that ravishing boy.

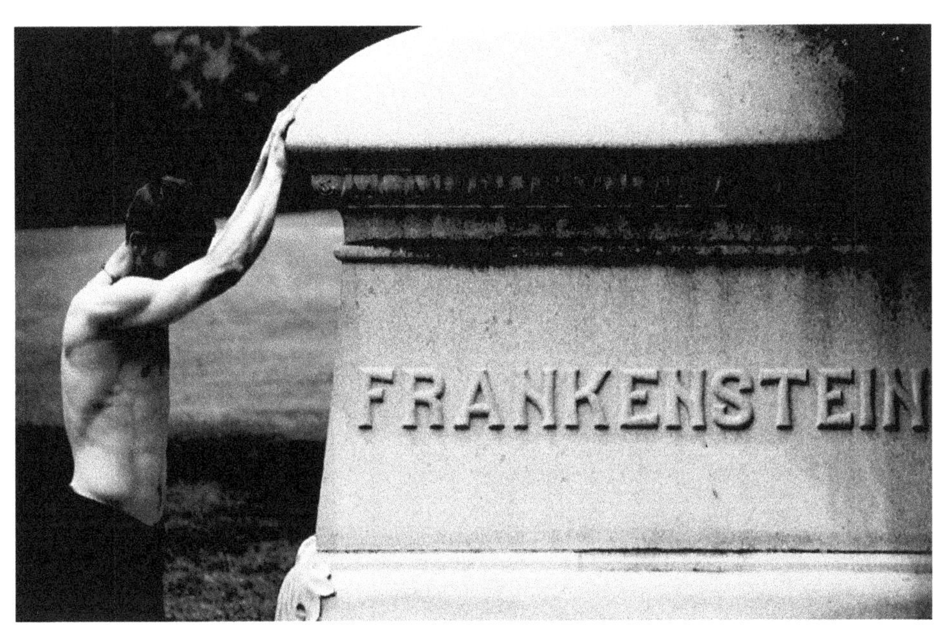

FRANKENSTEIN

Cumberland

Winged Hermes, winged Nike, the sun in his chariot,
Love's sudden flights to earth, even the phallos,
stony hard, is winged, and temple marble, heavy
as the mountains from which it's quarried, soars.
Art's a trick. Click. A bolt of wind-blown cloth's
a wing he holds with hand and arm, like a bit
of bird's bone, weightless as that, his body sky-
bound, eager to rise on no more than one wing.
Cumberland is five thousand miles from Greece.
His hair's grown-up shorn. Heaven's unsettled, fields
of dark clouds. Yet, save for earth's ring, the sky's
all his world, his ass beneath the feathery cloth
fine as any boy's or man's who would be borne
up on air like a bird stunned by the sun it's flying to.

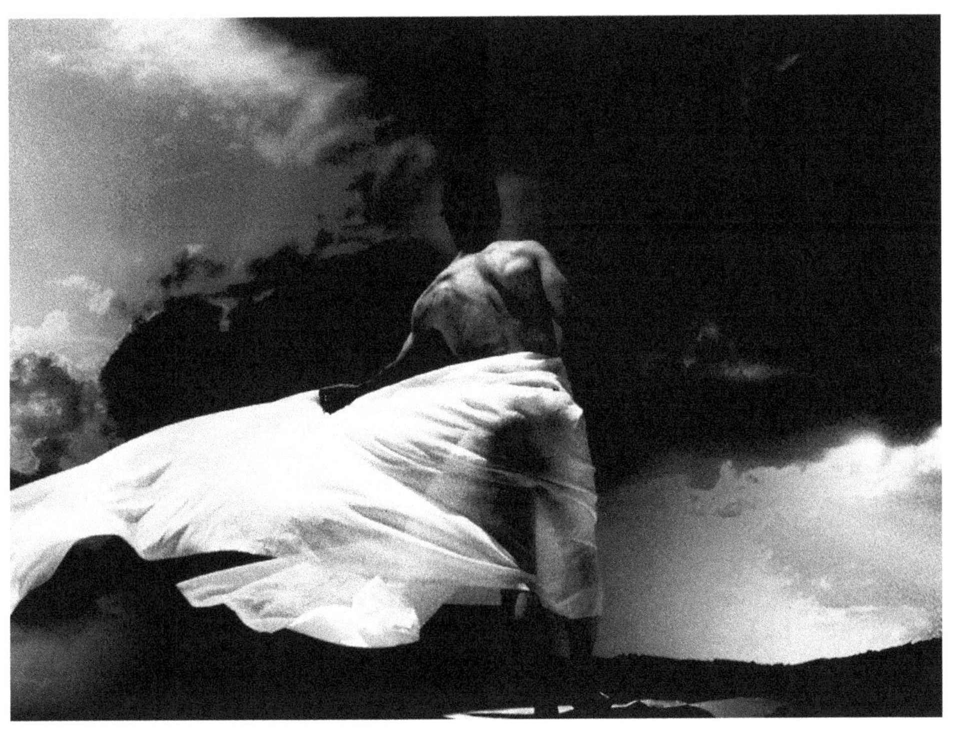

Pan III

A music that calls you by name, variations on
a monodic theme that enthralls you, entices
you to dance, to chant not hymns, but carnal
tunes you sing as if yours, the cave dark
yet lit by a lamp in that dream you dream:
the song of flesh, sex, the truth it proclaims,
its lyric games, the liberty to play. Let Be
be Seem, the ever changing always the same.
Or the Pan who calls you by name. Real,
the ring on his finger, the flute he holds,
his torso, his arms, his thighs, his cock daring
you not to abandon your dreams, the flame
he brings not a flickering in the back of a cave
but a flare that leads you to sunlight and seashores.

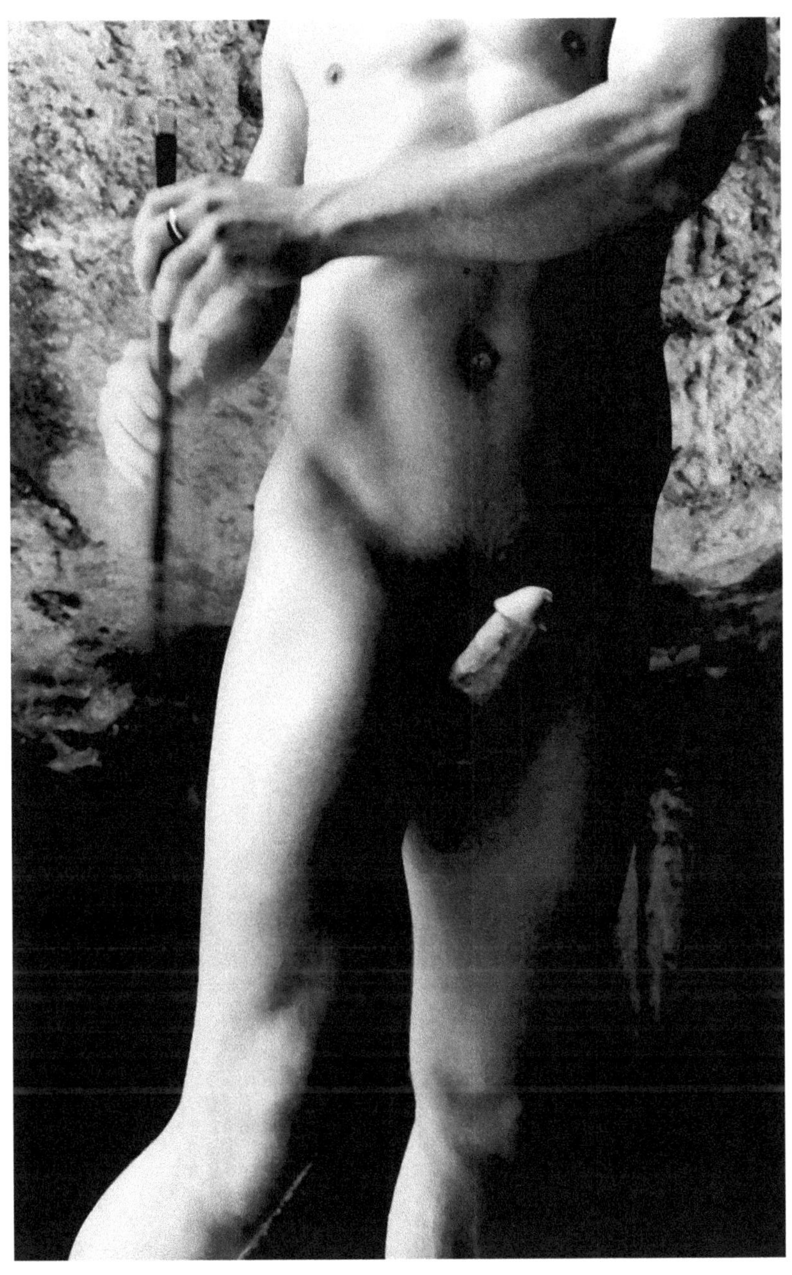

Prophet

Out of wilderness, he stands alone on the shore,
a place for departure and return. The rock's
black as his beard, the sand coarse, the water
dark, grand storm clouds an electric backdrop.
His robe's austere. He crooks his right arm,
unfolds his hand, and preaches to the sea.
Say paradise. A long ago day reborn from
dust, ash, clay, impossible but necessary,
the beach packed again, the sea full of swimmers.
The ancient bay is clearest blue. And handsome
men stand on the sand, safe once more. Say
paradise. Say may this vision prove true, a mercy
to the world, no fantasy but you and I playing
sunning dancing loving talking as then. Pray. Say paradise.

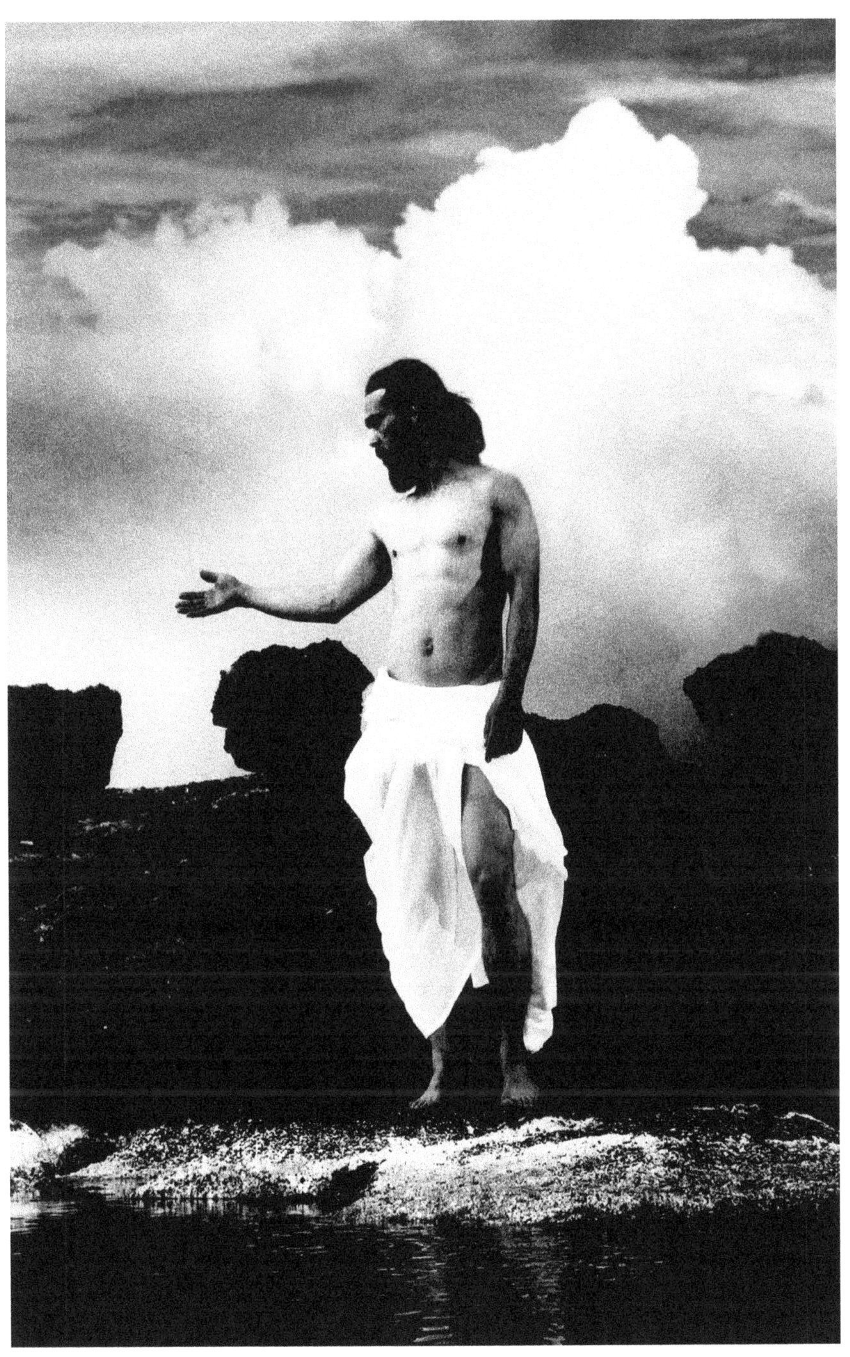

Peter Weltner was raised in suburban New Jersey and piedmont North Carolina. He received his A.B. from Hamilton College where he majored in English with a minor in Philosophy, and his Ph.D. in English from Indiana University. He taught for thirty-seven years in the English Department of San Francisco State, retiring in 2006. His first book of stories was published in 1989. His two novels, one collection of three short novels, four collections of short stories, and twenty or so books or chapbooks of poetry have been variously published by Five Fingers, The Crossing Press, Graywolf Press, Standing Stone Books, 2Rivers, Brick-House Books, Agenda Editions (UK), and Marrowstone, most recently The Lost Ghosts of Lemnos: Renderings and Renditions (2025). He's been awarded, among other literary honors, two O.Henry's and Fore-Word Magazine's Silver Award for fiction.

Galen Garwood is an American artist currently living in Northern Thailand. His creativity is expressed in various mediums: painting, monotypes, photography, digital art, filmmaking, and writing. His works have been exhibited in the US, Europe, and Asia. His multimedia piece "Adagio" won a Bronze Award at the International Multimedia Film Festival in Philadelphia, 1995, and in 1996 was included in the 1996 Venice Biennale's Xenograhia Nomadic Wall and again at Art Affair in New York. His film "Cadmium Red Ligh" was awarded First Place for Narrative/Documentary at the Port Townsend International Film Festival in 2007 and a First Place Award for Short Documentary for "Ed and Ed" at the DeReel Film Festival in Australia in 2008. He's collaborated with several poets, most notably Sam Hamill, Marvin Bell, and Peter Weltner. He is currently working on new paintings and his 'Galenographs,' a digital art form printed in physical editions as Giclee prints.